SHIRE NATURAL HI!

CW00919286

THE
BROWN HARE

STEPHEN TAPPER

CONTENTS

The European Brown Hare   2
Hare behaviour   6
Hare ecology 10
Conservation 19
Further reading 24

COVER: *Typical 'mad March hare' behaviour: a boxing match between two adults —
probably a female boxing off the attentions of a male.*

Series editors: Jim Flegg and Chris Humphries.

Set in 9 point Times roman and printed in Great Britain by C. I. Thomas & Sons
(Haverfordwest) Ltd, Press Buildings, Merlins Bridge, Haverfordwest, Dyfed.

The European Brown Hare

WHAT IS A HARE?

The non-zoologist might be forgiven for thinking that hares are basically large rodents with long ears and short tails. After all, they are herbivorous and have a prominent pair of incisors. Darwin made the same mistake and also classified them as rodents; however, taxonomists now consider that rabbits, hares and their allies are sufficiently distinct from the rodents to put them in a scparate order, the Lagomorpha. All rabbits, hares and the little known pikas are lagomorphs.

Lagomorphs have a number of characteristics which make them different from rodents. Behind the prominent front teeth of a rabbit or hare there is a second smaller pair. All lagomorphs have these and although they do not appear to be a vital part of their anatomy they are unique to lagomorphs: no rodent has this second set of teeth.

Another feature of much more importance is the lagomorph digestive system, which is specially adapted for eating grass and herbs. This food contains a large proportion of cellulose, which is difficult to digest and would normally pass through unused unless the animal has some method of breaking it down. Lagomorphs have a large sac, the *caecum*, which is morphologically equivalent to the human appendix and which contains bacteria and other micro-organisms capable of digesting the cellulose. In order to increase the efficiency of this digestion lagomorphs recycle the material back to their stomach. This is done by eating some of their own faeces. This behaviour, known as *refection*, is well developed in lagomorphs. Two types of faeces are produced: one, a soft oval lozenge is usually re-eaten directly from the anus; the other, a hard round pellet, is defaecated normally. Hares reingest the soft faeces during the day when they are resting, and the hard pellets are passed during the night when they are actively feeding.

Apart from these important internal features lagomorphs also look different from rodents. They all have rabbit-like faces with large wide eyes set high on the sides of their heads to give them all-round vision, and also a nose with a little closable flap which the animal opens and shuts — rabbits and hares are said to 'wink' their noses. Their ears are big but the head is supported only by a short weak neck. However, it is quite flexible and when at rest they can tuck their heads well back into their shoulders. All lagomorphs have thick soft fur, but their skin is not very tough and so their pelts have never been highly valued in the fur trade. Without exception their feet are fully furred top and bottom, and in the case of the North American Snowshoe Hare the fur is a highly developed mat which gives the animal broad feet for running on deep snow. Indeed, lagomorphs have adapted well to all climates and species are found from the tropics through to the Arctic even though no lagomorph is capable of hibernation.

Amongst the lagomorphs the pikas (Ochotonidae) are quite distinct. They are small hamster-like animals with short squat legs and have rounded ears rather than long pointed ones. There are a dozen or more species, most of which live in mountainous regions of Asia. There are no pikas in Europe but two species live in the alpine habitats of the North American Rockies. They are charming little creatures living amongst the rocks and boulders of high mountain rockslides. They forage on the adjacent alpine meadows and gather large haypiles under suitable rocks to serve as a winter food source.

The rest of the lagomorphs can be split broadly into rabbits and hares. The rabbit-like lagomorphs are less athletic than the hares and tend to live in burrows or warrens and not to forage far for their food; their young are born naked and blind (*altricial*) and are reared underground. Generally they escape predators by diving for their underground cover. Hares, on the other hand, are long-legged lanky animals living their life in open country. They forage over wide areas, have fully furred and sighted (*precocial*) young born in the open, and they

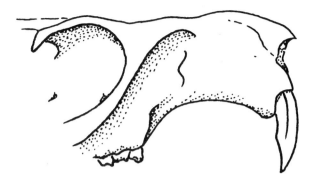

1. *A characteristic anatomical difference between rodents and lagomorphs is that skulls of the former have a single pair of large incisors (upper), whereas all lagomorphs have a small second set behind the main pair (lower, arrowed).*

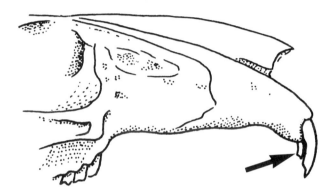

escape from predators by outrunning them.

In the British Isles there are two kinds of hare, the Blue or Mountain Hare (*Lepus timidus*) and the Brown or European Hare (*Lepus europaeus*). Mountain Hares, as the name implies, are upland animals living on the open moors and mountainsides of Scotland, the Peak District and North Wales. They feed on heather and other mountain plants and grow a winter coat of white or patchy white fur.

Brown Hares are common in most of England, Scotland and Wales, but until the nineteenth century were absent from Ireland. The Irish Hare is also *Lepus timidus* even though, unlike its cousin the Blue Hare, it keeps a brown coat all winter.

FIELD IDENTIFICATION

Compared to a rabbit an adult Brown Hare is large, a rabbit weighing 1.7 kg (3 pounds 12 ounces), a Brown Hare 3.5 kg (7 pounds 10 ounces). However, overall size is not the best guide to field identification: stature is far more recognisable, especially at a distance. Hares are tall and leggy in appearance and their gait when moving is quite distinct; they do not scamper off like rabbits but lope away or run with a well developed stride. At full gallop a Brown Hare reaches speeds of 55 to 70 km per hour (35 to 45 mph). Seen from the back, the hare's small tail, which is white below, is usually held downwards, showing its distinct black upper surface; a rabbit's tail shows as an all-white powder puff held upright as the animal runs, the black upper surface being invisible. A Mountain Hare does not have such a distinct black upper surface to its tail.

The Brown Hare's coat is quite brown, ranging from a foxy russet colour around the face, chest and flank, to a darker grizzled brown on the back: only on the belly is there a small area of white. In summer, the coat is overall a lighter colour and some animals take on a distinctly yellowish appearance. A rabbit is quite grey by comparison. A hare's ears have distinctly black tips and are much longer than those of a rabbit.

Unfortunately it is not possible to tell males from females in the field, although with a very powerful telescope the nipples of a lactating female might be seen. However, moult patterns and coat colour do vary considerably; with careful study, and combined with other features such as torn ears, it is possible to get to know the appearance of different individuals. In this way it is possible to study the social behaviour of some hares without having to use special marks such as ear tags.

HISTORY AND DISTRIBUTION

The Brown Hare is adapted to wide, open steppe country. With the retreat of the Quaternary ice and the development of the grass plains in Asia, the hare's habitat increased. In Britain the ice sheet left an Arctic tundra landscape and the first hares to take up residence were the *Lepus timidus* types. Indeed, it appears that Brown Hares spread north too late to get across the English Channel land bridge before it was cut by the rising sea level. It is not clear exactly when they did arrive, but there are no records of Brown Hares at any of the known pre-Roman sites. Thus it is quite probable that they were introduced by the Romans. Agriculture and its associated forest clearance were already under way by the time the first Brown Hare appeared. Hares were well suited to the new arable farmland since it was so similar to their native habitat.

In historic times the hare's fortunes have been closely associated with agricultural development, and wherever man has cleared the forest and created arable farmland hares have moved in soon after. This has continued to happen in quite recent times: in central Russia, as forests were cleared along the route of the trans-Siberian railway, new farming communities developed and hares spread eastwards. Much the same process must have taken place in Britain with Brown Hares moving into almost every corner of the isles as man developed the farming. Only the uplands and mountains remained uncolonised, perhaps due to the presence of the already established

2. *European Brown Hares have a wide geographical distribution across Europe and Asia. Related forms occur in Spain and Africa.*

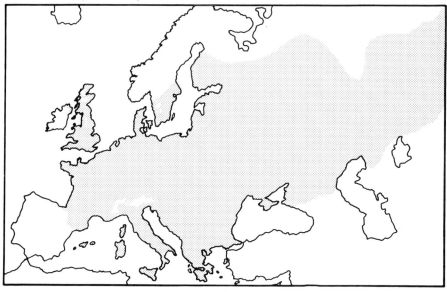

3 (above). *A pika from the Rocky Mountains in Canada. Pikas, like hares, are lagomorphs but belong to a different family, the Ochotonidae.*

4 (right). *Rabbits are in the same family as hares but are colonial burrowers.*

Mountain Hare. Although they spread to most of the British Isles they did not reach Ireland, and there the Irish Hare has remained common in uplands and lowlands. However, during the nineteenth century Brown Hares were extensively introduced into Ireland for hare coursing, and it remains to be seen whether or not the descendants of these animals will spread and replace the Irish Hare over much of its range. At present they seem to be well established only in parts of Counties Tyrone and Sligo in the north.

It is not known how common hares were in these earlier times, but it is likely that they reached a peak of abundance during the Victorian era of high arable farming. In those times the pattern of farming, in which cereal crops rotated with turnips and grass and clover leys left for hay, provided hares with continuous good forage all year round. In addition, the developing fashion for game shooting ensured that the hare's natural predators, already hunted down by farmers to protect their livestock, also faced the determined efforts of some 25,000 gamekeepers intent on killing anything that could prey on partridges or pheasants. Without doubt the hare benefited from this intensive predator control and game-shooting records indicate that hares have never been as common as they were in the 1890s and 1900s. Hares remain common in more arable areas, but newer farming methods do not suit them so well and they might disappear from some districts if they are not specially conserved.

Hare behaviour

HARE ACTIVITY

Unlike species which go underground when inactive, hares remain above ground in daylight hours, and it is easy to forget that they are mainly nocturnal animals, actively feeding at night and resting by day. However, summer nights are short, so much of their activity extends into the early mornings and begins before dusk. Hares active in the middle of the day have usually been disturbed.

Hares living on farmland rest in fields where there is good all-round visibility. If the crop is long enough to hide its body the hare will do no more than squat down and remain still. If the vegetation is short or the weather is cold and windy, it may dig a *form* into which it can sink its hindquarters — out of sight and sheltered from the weather. Hares are almost invisible when resting in their forms. A field of winter wheat, where the ground is rolled flat and the corn only an inch or two high, may look as bare and smooth as a bowling green; but as the sun goes down hares may be seen to emerge from shallow depressions all over the field, stretch themselves and begin feeding. A hare returning to a form in the early morning appears to melt back into the ground as it begins its rest period. Not all hares rest in open fields; a surprising number choose to retreat to a nearby wood or copse, especially in winter. Watch the edges of some woods in this season and the murky outlines of dozens of hares can be seen coming out after dark to feed.

Feeding areas may be close to the form and the animal may simply get up and begin feeding at once. Commonly, however, good feeding areas and suitable resting sites are not in the same place and a hare will have to travel perhaps up to a kilometre (1000 yards) to get to a suitable crop. Once at a feeding spot, hares will generally stay in the same area most of the night. We often think of hares as being solitary animals — indeed many of the early natural history books described them as such. But this is not the case: they prefer to be in loosely aggregated groups, especially when feeding. Presumably a group of hares is better able to spot an approaching predator than a single animal with its one pair of eyes and ears. Research has shown that hares feeding in groups can spend more time actually feeding and less looking around than if they are alone. Feeding areas change as crops grow and are harvested and fields are ploughed; thus an animal will have to shift feeding areas from field to field in a

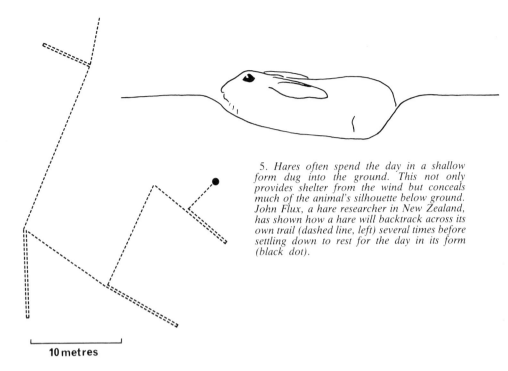

5. *Hares often spend the day in a shallow form dug into the ground. This not only provides shelter from the wind but conceals much of the animal's silhouette below ground. John Flux, a hare researcher in New Zealand, has shown how a hare will backtrack across its own trail (dashed line, left) several times before settling down to rest for the day in its form (black dot).*

10 metres

seasonal manner. The area over which it can make its living in this way can vary from 20 to 100 ha (50 to 250 acres) depending on the type of farm. This is the animal's home range, which it will know intimately. Its familiarity with gaps in hedges or fences, changes in the slope of the ground and the location of thick cover will all be important to help the animal escape rapidly from predators and will enable it to exploit the resources of the area efficiently.

Techniques for avoiding predators are particularly important and hares take a number of precautions to minimise predation risk. When returning to their forms they will often backtrack two or three times to confuse the trail for a scent-hunting predator. Some observations also suggest that hares may have a 'race track', which they can use to speed away from a pursuing carnivore. This race track is a specific route, every twist and turn of which the hare knows well, and over which it will have practised running at full speed several times. Presumably, if chased by a predator it can

get on to this race track and then run as fast as possible without worrying about misfooting or hitting obstacles. Hares are very adept at avoiding capture even by dogs like greyhounds which have been specially bred for speed and can outpace a hare over a short distance. A greyhound set after a hare will catch it up in the first hundred or so yards, but just as the dog is almost on top of it the hare will turn sharply to one side leaving the dog to charge on in the wrong direction. Once it has done this two or three times the dog, which usually has less stamina than the hare, will often give up. Alternatively, the hare may run along the length of a hedge or other cover, and then make its sharp dodge directly in front of a gap, so it can slip away out of sight just as the dog goes racing past.

SOCIAL BEHAVIOUR AND COURTSHIP

Although hares are social in the sense that they prefer to be in groups, their society is not complicated. They do not hold territories or go through ritualistic

6 (above). *Mountain Hares are close relatives of the Brown Hare and are found in moorland areas of Scotland and the Peak District.*

7 (left). *A typical adult Brown Hare in summer pelage; notice its huge hind feet and long ears with black tips.*

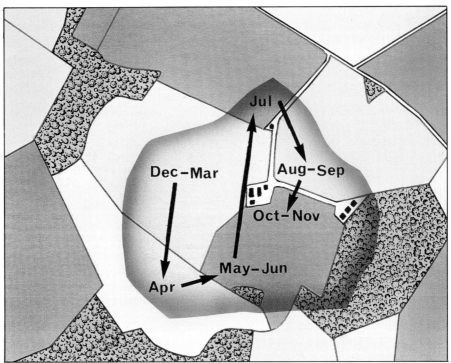

8. *A hare's home range (outlined in red) on an arable farm can be between 20 and 100 hectares (50 to 250 acres). Feeding areas are switched from field to field as crops grow and provide fresh forage. This animal used a winter wheat field from December to March, spent April in spring barley but moved on to a grass ley when the barley became too long. Livestock forced it to switch to another grass field in July, but by August it was finding fresh forage on a winter barley stubble that had been drilled with turnip for later sheep grazing. By October the turnip was too long to feed on and the hare had returned to the grass ley.*

displays to attract mates and deter rivals. There are no female harems owned by especially large males, neither is there a rigid pair-bonding system to which all animals adhere. However, studies of wild hares are beginning to show that there is more of a pattern to their social organisation than was at first realised. It has been shown, for example, that at choice feeding sites more dominant animals may drive away younger or less assertive ones, and in some instances a loose dominance hierarchy may develop. Competition for food is unusual since on farmland food comes in field-size units: when a crop provides forage there is more than enough for those hares in the area. However, receptive females are always in

short supply for the adult males and competition for mating can sometimes be intense.

Hares are polygynous and a male may mate with any number of females. When the breeding season starts, usually towards the end of January or in early February as hares are coming into reproductive condition, males will pay considerable attention to the females. At this time hares will often be seen following one another around, and mate guarding, whereby a male will station himself close by a female and chase off other males, will develop. A male chasing off another male will simply run at it and, if it gets close enough, give it a sharp bite. As a female nears oestrus the male in attend-

9

ance will pay more and more attention to her, sniffing the ground after her as she moves about feeding. If he chivvies her too much she will eventually get irritated and turn on him, boxing at him with her forepaws. This is typical spring behaviour and accounts for the 'mad March hare' stories. It was believed that boxing matches were fights between rival males but now it has been established that they are almost always the result of females, which on average are larger and heavier than males, fending off the advances of too amorous males. Eventually the female will allow the male to approach and mount her; copulation takes place quickly, often ending with the male giving a little jump away. Mating is not confined to March or early spring but continues all through the long breeding season until about September. However, it is much more noticeable in spring because most females come into breeding condition together for the first time; also crops and grass fields are short at this time and hare activity is easily seen.

Once mating has taken place the male will start to look for another female. Competition for females is intense, and a successful dominant male will be able to mate with a large proportion of the local females. A younger and less dominant male may associate with a female and may guard her for a while; however, as she approaches full oestrus it is likely that a dominant male will chase him off. Frequently the result is several hares all tagging along behind one female. Although there seems to be a loose ranking system amongst the males when it comes to breeding, there is no evidence yet that there is anything of this kind amongst females. They seem to space themselves out over the suitable habitat but there is no suggestion that they fight for the space available.

Leverets are born in the open and initially hidden together in cover. Within a few days they will move to separate forms nearby to minimise the risk of predation. Young are born fully furred and with their eyes open and need a minimum of looking after by the female. Indeed she keeps her visits to them down to the shortest possible time so their whereabouts are not revealed. Lactation is restricted to one brief period every 24 hours. This lactation is normally only a five-minute period one hour after sunset. The female will return to the place where the young were born and the young leverets will gather round and suckle. Occasionally the place and time may be altered slightly if the area is disturbed in some way. Young leverets seem to have an innate behaviour for following at this time, and any strange hare may be trailed if it happens into this suckling area: indeed young leverets not only follow one another around but have also been observed to pursue other species such as Lapwings. Female hares do not seem to be particular about which leverets they suckle, and when two or more litters are present in the same area it is not unusual for leverets to get mixed and a female to nurse her neighbour's youngsters.

Hare ecology

GROWTH AND REPRODUCTION

At birth an average leveret weighs about 100 grams (3½ ounces) and may reach adult weight after about six months. Although animals born early in the summer will attain adult weight and reach sexual maturity in the same season, it is unusual in Britain for them to breed during the year of their birth. The breeding season is very extended in hares and normally lasts from mid February to mid September; however, there is a good deal of variation in the length of season from year to year, depending on summer weather. A warm spring will cause an early onset, and an Indian summer will considerably extend the reproductive period. In Scotland, over thirteen years, the season was found to vary between 176 and 344 days. Weather affects breeding performance as well as season length. In warm summers a greater proportion of females are pregnant at any one time and they tend to produce larger litters. Year to year variation in the numbers of young produced is therefore large.

Females can have up to four litters a year, but three is more usual. Three-year-

10

old females are the most productive, older and younger animals being less fecund. Pregnancy begins when the female ovulates four to five eggs in response to mating. This induced form of ovulation, typical of rabbits and hares, ensures a high fertility rate. Hares also ovulate very soon after giving birth and occasionally may even ovulate before parturition, so that rarely females may be found with two ages of embryos in their uteri. Some of the embryos may be lost during pregnancy, but except early in the season or for diseased hares these losses are not significant. The litter size will vary according to season: in early spring it may be one or two; later in the summer it may be three or four. Pregnancy lasts for 41 to 42 days and after the young are born the female will nurse them for a period between 20 and 30 days. This lactation is normally terminated by the arrival of the next litter, but at the end of the breeding season the last remaining leverets may continue to be nursed for several more weeks.

LIFE EXPECTANCY AND SURVIVAL

In Poland, where there has been much research on hare ecology, a large number of young leverets were tagged and their numbers followed for many years. The longest surviving animal lived to twelve years. This, though an exceptional occurrence, can be taken as the maximum possible life span of a hare. Normally an animal of five years would be considered old, and on British farmland, where the mortality rate is normally high, three or four years is the normal maximum. Since the death rate is high, life expectancy is short: for a healthy adult hare it is only just over a year. So of the adult hares alive in any one year only half of them are likely to be alive next year. Hare populations make up for this high loss by prolific breeding, and after a good summer more than half of the over-wintering population will consist of young animals. Causes of mortality range from the natural factors of disease and predation to the man-made ones of pesticide poisoning, shooting and road traffic losses.

Hares get a number of different dis-eases, including myxomatosis, the lethal virus which has periodically swept through rabbit populations since it was introduced by man in 1954. However, it is very unusual in hares and it does not cause any measurable loss to the population as a whole. Dermatitis is more noticeable and many people mistake this for myxomatosis. The affected animal has lesions or scabby areas of skin, usually around the face and genital areas. Dermatitis does not affect the population seriously. However, two other diseases, coccidiosis and yersiniosis, sweep through populations in epidemics which can kill large numbers of hares. Cocci-diosis is caused by an enormous increase in the *Eimeria* protozoans, which normally reside in the digestive tract of hares in small numbers. Affected hares develop lesions on their internal organs and they quickly become thin and die. Leverets and young hares are most affected by this disease as they have little time to build up the natural immunity which adults develop. Wet weather increases the disease, and in a wet autumn following a dry summer a lot of young hares will succumb to the first wave of coccidiosis. Farmers often report finding them dead in quite large numbers at this time of the year. Yersiniosis, by contrast, seems to affect mainly adult hares, quite often in the spring. Animals affected die very quickly without loss of weight and when picked up dead are apparently in good bodily condition.

Adult hares because of their size and speed are usually quite adept at avoiding predation. Leverets are exceedingly vulnerable as they are in the open from birth. Although birds of prey like owls frequently take leverets, the main natural enemy of the hare is the fox. Remains of hare carcases are commonly found near fox earths, and studies of foxes in country areas show them to have a large proportion of hares in their diet. However, it is not always possible to tell whether the hare that a fox has eaten was killed and not scavanged by the fox. In Europe there is circumstantial evidence that predation by foxes is holding down the hare numbers. In Germany rabies periodically decimates parts of the fox population, and in these places hare numbers increase

9 (above). *A female hare is guarded by a male (behind). Mate guarding is a common behaviour as females approach oestrus.*
10 (below). *Males scrap over a female. Tony Holley, a hare researcher in Somerset, observed this female crouching as a guarding male behind is challenged by another facing the camera.*
11 (opposite). *A female boxes off the attentions of an over-amorous male.*

significantly for a year or two afterwards. However, we still have a considerable amount to learn about the significance of predation to hare populations.

To these natural mortalities man has added new losses with his latest technological farming methods. Farm machinery is now faster and more dangerous than it was before the Second World War. Grass cutters, which were formerly slow horse-drawn gadgets used for haymaking, have been replaced by fast-moving tractor-drawn mowers or forage harvesters. These can easily catch an unsuspecting leveret and incorporate it into the silage. Stubble fields used to be weedy and provide the hare population with autumn forage for the coming winter. Nowadays this stubble together with the straw is likely to be burnt and leverets may get burnt as well. Sprays are another hazard hares did not have to contend with in earlier days. Today a cereal crop may be treated with more than a dozen sprays including herbicides, fungicides and insecticides, and today's long spray booms probably spray the hare directly as it lies hidden in the crop. The effect of all these agrochemicals on the hares is largely unknown but at least one herbicide, paraquat, is known to be lethal even in very dilute concentrations. It is, moreover, a chemical which is very popular with farmers, since it is a fast-acting weed killer that can be applied to autumn stubble fields to get rid of persistent arable weeds and germinating seedlings from the previous crop. With this chemical the process of cultivation and autumn drilling can proceed with the minimum of delay. Unfortunately these weedy stubbles are very attractive to hares and they can be death traps where this herbicide is extensively used. Other agricultural effects may be more subtle and may be the cause of the reduced hare numbers found on some farmland areas in recent times.

Road deaths are another hazard of modern times. Dead hares are a common sight on many country roads and they are particularly vulnerable to fast-moving traffic. Hares often have to cross roads to get to feeding areas from their daytime resting places. In addition wide roadside verges may prove to be attractive feeding areas in themselves, particularly when the other crops are too mature to be palatable. The normal response of a hare to danger is not to duck into a hole but to run away at full speed, and this is no use when the pursuing predator is an onrushing car.

POPULATIONS

The numbers of hares on farmland differ widely across Britain. In some areas they are entirely absent, whereas in other places they are so common as to be an agricultural pest. The cause of these differences is not always clear: often the farming methods are apparently similar in the two areas. Nevertheless arable farmland in general supports a higher density of hares than pastureland. However, there are many arable areas with few hares, and disturbingly these areas appear to be increasing. There are no nationwide surveys of hare numbers and almost the only source of information on long-term changes in their abundance comes from farm and estate shooting records. These are not ideal, being based on the numbers of hares killed, not the number alive, but they have one big advantage in that they are often based on traditional hare shoots, which in many areas have been carried out annually on the same piece of ground for a century or more. When bag records from a group of estates are averaged they give a useful index of hare abundance both regionally and annually. These records indicate that hare abundance has dropped markedly since about 1960, with the biggest reduction in numbers occurring in the late 1960s.

We can only speculate about what may have caused this large decline as there has been little research on hares in Britain and there have been many changes in agriculture during this time. One important but subtle change that has taken place in farming methods over this time is the scale of arable and particularly cereal farming. On farmland, to obtain an adequate year-round food supply a hare must shift its feeding areas from field to field as some crops become mature and unpalatable and other ones in their younger stages provide suitable forage. Always, winter and summer, the hare is looking for short young growth which is nutritious and easily digested. The old-fashioned methods of cereal farming provided an ideal landscape for hares. Fields were small, so hares did not have far to go to get to the next crop, and cereals were always rotated with other crops, so that no field remained in a single crop for more than a year or two. A crop of winter wheat might be followed by spring barley for the next two years; the second crop of barley would be undersown with a grass and clover mix, which would be left to grow through the cereal stubble after harvest to create a ley pasture. These leys might be used for hay the following year as well as pasture for sheep and cattle. Ley grass could be left down for two to three years before being ploughed in for drilling another crop of winter wheat. Such a system always provided hares with suitable forage at any time of the year — a patchwork quilt landscape in which hares never had to travel far for food. In winter and early spring wheat provided the lush new growth; by late spring, when the wheat was getting too long, spring barley supplied another suitable forage area. By mid-summer, when all cereals are too tall for food, ley meadows provided an alternative rich in herbs and grasses. Even after harvest these leys, together with the new ones established by undersowing, kept the food supply going until the winter corn came through in midwinter.

Today cereal growing has been greatly simplified, largely to the detriment of the

12. *The national average numbers of hares shot each year by farmers has been declining since the early 1960s. This probably reflects a declining live population as well. (Data from the Game Conservancy's National Game Census.)*

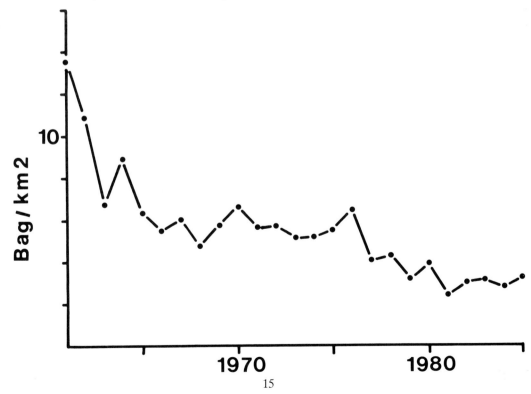

13. *This young leveret has been disturbed by grass mowing in the field in which it was hiding.*
14. *Stubbles with stooks usually contained a lot of weeds which provided excellent food for hares in late summer.*

15 (above) and 16 (below). *Straw burning not only removes potential feeding areas for hares but can also kill leverets.*

17

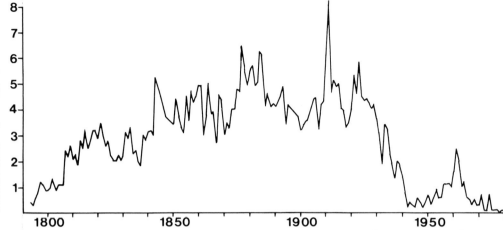

17. *The bag record from a large Norfolk estate not only reflects the changing fortunes of the hare but also shows the extent to which the numbers shot varied from year to year as a result of variable breeding success.*

hare. To accommodate bigger tractors and other farm machines fields have been greatly enlarged. Large fields help the farmer since the number of turns the tractor makes is greatly reduced. In modern crops which require many chemical applications this is a significant saving. This does not help a hare, which will have much further to travel between feeding fields. Indeed hares in these landscapes have larger home ranges than those on small, more diversified farms. Modern cereal growing no longer requires a rotation of crops; they can be grown for continuous periods on the same ground, and if a break is needed oilseed rape or beans are used. These crops provide no substitute food for hares since they are sown and harvested at roughly the same time as the cereals. This may mean that in some areas the entire landscape is cleared and cultivated in September, leaving nothing but bare soil from one horizon to the other until the winter-sown crops begin to appear in late November. It is not surprising that in such areas hares are often found dead or dying at this time and that farmland of this type generally does not support a high population.

Apart from farming, there are natural factors which have reduced hare abundance. The most obvious one is the weather. We have already seen that it has an enormous influence on breeding performance: a succession of wet cold summers could reduce production, and this in turn would lead to fewer hares being shot and eventually to lower overall numbers. Meteorological records for the last 25 years suggest that the reduction in numbers could be partly accounted for by poor breeding performance due to adverse weather. Another factor which appears to have contributed to this decline is the dramatic change in the rabbit population. After 1954, when myxomatosis killed off 99.9 per cent of Britain's rabbits, hare numbers began to increase and by 1961 they seemed to have peaked. Thus the gradual reduction in hares since the mid 1960s could, in part, also be the end of a sudden irruption in the early 1960s, with perhaps a further reduction as rabbit populations gradually recovered. However, such an attractive explanation seems unlikely. Hares have declined throughout much of Europe in a very similar fashion to Great Britain. In Denmark, a country where rabbits are almost entirely absent, bag records show a decline virtually identical to Britain's. The post-myxomatosis effect must therefore have been only for a few years in the late 1950s and early 1960s. It is the intensification of farming across most of northern Europe which has had most impact on hare numbers.

Conservation

RELATIONS WITH MAN

It is hardly surprising that an animal which spends almost its entire life in open fields and most of its active time eating crops is considered an agricultural pest. However, farmers are usually quite tolerant of hares and either fail to notice or overlook a lot of the damage they do. Unlike rabbits, which graze within a short distance of their burrows and so eat out a whole swath of crop beside a hedge or along the edge of a wood, hares shift about in the middle of fields and therefore their damage is in little patches and may often pass unnoticed when the crop is viewed from the track. Another reason is that the hare is the very embodiment of wildlife on an arable farm; most farmers like to see them around and enjoy watching their antics in the spring and summer months. If a farmer considers them too plentiful he will feel justified in organising a hare shoot to reduce the population substantially. This is normally held in February, when most other game shooting is finished, and when most hares will be sitting out on the winter corn. Usually between twenty and forty people with shotguns are needed so that a group of fields can be surrounded; as people move inwards gradually enclosing the hares animals are shot as they try to escape the cordon. Such methods can reduce the population by up to 60 per cent. However, a vigorous hare population can quickly recover from this loss and breeding success may increase as result of the reduced density. In areas where hares are very abundant hare shoots are annual events, but with the decline in hare numbers many shoots have been stopped. Where numbers are not excessive there is no need for an annual hare shoot, and if the population is not very productive as a result of modern farming a large-scale hare shoot could wipe them out completely. However, there will still be occasions when an animal will do something particularly annoying, such as eating a whole row of lettuces in a vegetable plot

18. *These hares shot on a February hare shoot in Hampshire will be sold to game dealers but may end up in kitchens and restaurants in Britain or Germany.*

19. *A pack of beagles meets at a south of England pub.*
20. *The slipper lets two greyhounds off the leash at a coursing meet.*

or, during snow conditions when there is little food around, cutting down and eating the tops from the new young trees planted for a future spinney or shelter belt. On these occasions the hare is usually shot.

Although the hare is not a major agricultural pest it is an important game animal. In continental Europe the hare is regarded as the most important of all small game, although British sportsmen prefer shooting driven grouse or pheasants to hares. However, hares are tasty animals to eat, and a considerable number are taken for the pot. It is as a quarry for hounds that the British hare is most highly prized. No doubt this is because it is very visible, prefers to escape over open country, has a great turn of speed when pressed and has considerable stamina. There are two different kinds of hounds which are used to hunt hares. Beagles are like small foxhounds and are hunted as a pack, with the dogs either flushing a hare and following its fresh trail by scent, or coming across the trail where an animal has recently passed. Beagles are very slow dogs (this is essential as the huntsmen are usually on foot rather than on horseback) and have little chance of killing a hare initially. To make up for this, they have tremendous perseverance and they aim to catch their quarry by wearing it down. Packs of beagles kill very few hares and their impact on the numbers in any local area can be considered trivial. Hunts with beagles can often be carried out successfully in areas where hares are not particularly numerous, indeed too many hares tend to confuse the pack. Hare coursing, on the other hand, usually requires a high local population before it can take place at all.

A formal hare coursing event is a knockout competition between pairs of greyhounds or a similar breed of dog. The object of each contest is not to kill the hare but for each dog to outperform its opponent by taking the lead in the chase and taking the initiative in such manoeuvres as turning the hare. The day is organised round a coursing field on which the dogs can run, usually a grass ley or stubble. Spectators are aligned along two opposite sides of the field, and one end is adjacent to another field where a large number of hares are known to be lying up. It is along this edge that hares will enter the coursing field, and concealed along it will be the dog handler or slipper. He releases the dogs when both animals have seen the hare and in his judgement given the hare an adequate start. The far end of the field is either open or has a fence or hedge which allows hares to slip out of sight of the dogs. Once the dogs lose sight of their quarry they give up. Hares are driven on to the coursing area by a semicircle of beaters in the neighbouring field who will try to flush them forward one at a time. Contrary to popular belief the hares are not held captive and released out of boxes in front of dogs but are wild ones that live in the local area. Furthermore the slipper takes care that the dogs are set after fit adult hares and not sick ones or leverets. The majority of hares escape after being coursed, but a proportion (usually about one in five) are caught and killed by the hounds.

Hunting animals is a controversial subject but hare coursing is one of the oldest field sports, with a clear set of rules and traditions. Because the sport requires a high hare population, coursing supporters have always been a force for hare conservation, encouraging farmers to leave stubbles over winter and to be careful with the use of agrochemicals, and above all in trying to dissuade them from organising hare shoots.

Unregulated hare coursing is usually poaching and is a growing menace in the countryside. The growing fashion for 'long dogs' or lurchers (greyhounds crossed with other breeds) inevitably leads many owners into the temptation of setting them after hares. Apart from the hares they kill, it is perversely causing many farmers to decide that having hares on their farm is tempting trespassers on to their land. Consequently they make a determined effort to get rid of any resident hares they may have left.

CONSERVATION ON FARMLAND

Conservation of any species consists of two separate strategies: increasing the 'carrying capacity' and improving survival.

21. *A long-net is used to catch a hare for radio-tracking. Once captured it is given a lightweight collar which contains a miniature radio, allowing the research workers to determine exactly where it is day and night.*

22. *A vehicle-mounted directional aerial is used to pinpoint the location of a radio-collared hare. By means of these modern research methods a lot has been learnt about the hare's needs on farmland.*

23. *New shelter belts like this one give extra cover and food for hares in a landscape that would be quite bare after harvest.*

Carrying capacity is the ability of the habitat to support the species in question. The greater the carrying capacity of the landscape the more hares it will support. It is this carrying capacity that must be increased, if we want more hares. Hares need both food and cover from the landscape. The first is essential and the second desirable, for although hares can survive in landscapes with little or no cover they will use it if it is provided. Cover gives shelter from the worst of the elements, and windproof crops such as roots, fodder rape or stubble turnips give good cover at a time of the year when cereals are absent. However, permanent cover is better: hedgerows, small woods, rough banks and corners all help to provide shade in summer and shelter in winter. A wide low hedge with a bank of thick tall grass is ideal for hares (as well as other game animals like partridges). This cover needs to be distributed throughout the farm in small pockets and not concentrated at one end. If new cover is being created, then shelter belts and game spinneys are excellent. However, when establishing new trees it may be necessary to protect them from damage by hares as well as rabbits; tree guards or tree shelters are ideal for this. Rabbit netting will simply fence the hares out. When providing cover it should be remembered that hares like an open landscape. They do not like to be hemmed in by trees for they rely for their safety on seeing approaching predators in good time: small fields with overhanging hedges will give rise to too many ambush situations.

A consistent food supply is the most important factor in ensuring a flourishing hare stock, but a field that happens to be green is not necessarily suitable for hares to feed in. Hares like short growing crops and, unless there is an abundance of weeds, full-grown cereals or other crops will be of little use. The key factor in relation to food for hares is continuity; without this hares are likely to face an acute food shortage at some time during the year. Hares carry very little fat and have to solve their nutritional requirements on a day to day basis. It is the late summer and autumn that are usually the problem periods and any forage which fills the gap between harvest and the emergence of winter cereals in November is very valuable. Stubbles are ideal since they will be a rich source of wild grasses and herbs. If fields destined for spring crops can be left unploughed until late winter then they will provide excellent food sources for hares. Short grass provides a very useful buffer against other food supply fluctuations. If one wishes to increase food in an area devoid of forage at some time of the year, it can be provided best as a long grass strip, such as a gallop for horses. This could be a lifeline of food in an area that otherwise would be an autumn desert.

Increasing the survival of hares is largely a matter of being careful to avoid the farming hazards which often kill them; grass cutting, crop spraying and stubble burning are all practices which lead to hare deaths and many of the accidents are caused by the job being done too fast and not allowing time for hares to slip away. Stubble and straw burns in particular should be done slowly into the wind and not started with a wide encircling drive around the headlands lighting up all sides at once. If stubbles must be sprayed with paraquat before ploughing it should be done on a dry morning, not on a damp evening just before hares become active.

Natural losses to the population cannot be avoided but they can be reduced. A good, well dispersed and continuous food supply will reduce losses from disease, and good cover in summer is likely to reduce predation losses.

CONCLUSION

The fate of the hare rests almost wholly with Britain's farmers. Hares do not survive in urban or suburban areas; woodlands are unsuitable except as cover, and most nature reserves are far too small to support good populations. It is essential that farms are kept not only as flourishing businesses, but also as part of a hospitable landscape for wildlife. If farms become food factories there will be no place for hares. We have already seen evidence that numbers have dwindled, and if this continues hares will cease to be common countryside animals. Protection in law would do nothing to help; if a farmer cannot protect his crops or shoot a hare for the pot he might well decide he could do without them altogether. Hare conservation will work only if farmers can be encouraged to take steps to maintain and improve their farms for wildlife.

Further reading

Corbet, G. B., and Southern, H. N. *The Handbook of British Mammals*. The Mammal Society, Blackwells, Oxford, 1977.
Evans, G. E., and Thompson, D. *The Leaping Hare*. Faber and Faber, 1972.

ACKNOWLEDGEMENTS

I am most grateful to Tony Holley for the use of his superb photographs and also for help with the manuscript. Thanks are also due to Dick Potts for suggestions on the text. Illustrations are acknowledged to: the British Field Sports Society, 19, 20; the Game Conservancy, 15, 16, 21, 23; Tony Holley, 9, 10, 11; Chris Knights, 4, 6; Silvestris-Meyers, cover, 7. All other illustrations are by the author.